GO SET A WATCHMAN

A SIDEKICK

TO THE HARPER LEE NOVEL

by

ALLISON CLARE THEVENY

Published by

WeLoveNovels

I

II

Disclaimer: This publication is an unofficial Sidekick to *Go Set a Watchman* and does not contain the novel. It is designed for fiction enthusiasts who are reading the novel, or have just finished. Order a copy of the novel *Go Set a Watchman* on Amazon.

WeLoveNovels maintains an independent voice in delivering critical analysis and commentary; we are not affiliated with or endorsed by the publisher or author of *Go Set a Watchman*.

Questions? Ideas? Comments?

Email founders@welovenovels.com.

We are listening!

IV

Table of Contents

INTRODUCTION   7

EXPLORING THE AUTHOR'S FICTIONAL WORLD   13

CHAPTER ANALYSIS & DISCUSSION   17

CHARACTER GUIDE   39

A CLOSER LOOK: 41

IMAGINING ALTERNATE ENDINGS   47

THEMES & SYMBOLS YOU MAY HAVE MISSED   51

WATCHMAN'S CONTROVERSY IN TODAY'S PUBLISHING INDUSTRY   57

THE BIG PICTURE: WHAT CAN WE TAKE AWAY FROM THIS NOVEL?   61

POSSIBLE STORYLINES FOR A PREQUEL   65

IN THE FINAL ANALYSIS . . .   69

IF YOU LOVED THIS NOVEL . . .   73

ABOUT THE AUTHOR OF THIS SIDEKICK   78

Introduction

Hot anger you can't control as a brother cheats at your favorite game, the instant, unquestioned intimacy of whispering your whole heart and soul to a friend while sleeping in your secret fort, the warm security of gripping your father's hand, broken only by the sudden rush of seeming danger as he swings you up onto his shoulders. Childhood impressions might last a lifetime, but sooner or later, we all grow up.

Or so Harper Lee's *Go Set a Watchman* seems to suggest. Much like the unusual story behind its recent publication, however, *Watchman* does not just take *To Kill a Mockingbird*'s coming-of-age narrative one step further by showing us the reluctant, imperfect lady that young tomboy Scout (now Jean Louise) has become. While *Watchman* reads like a sequel to *Mockingbird* in that it depicts what happens when the now twenty-six-year-old protagonist returns to her Alabama hometown, Lee has described the new work as a "parent" to the original tale. Lee wrote *Watchman* first, and when she submitted it to her editor, the editor suggested that she build a new story out of the childhood sequences found in her first draft. She did, and the result was *To Kill a Mockingbird*.

Thus *Watchman*, whether you consider it as a template for *Mockingbird* or a story in its own right, does more than depict a protagonist's journey from child to adult. It questions the grownups and the parents we label as such. It makes us wonder if we should have followed Peter Pan's lead, gripped our father's hands a little longer, and read *Mockingbird* over and over, knowing that even if its cover fell off and its pages tore that its good guys would stay the good guys.

This may be a cryptic introduction to *Go Set a Watchman*, but much about this story, including its publication, its plot, and its differences from *Mockingbird*, evokes mystery, uncertainty, and, for many critics, disappointment. Even if you have not read *To Kill a Mockingbird* (which, fear not, isn't required reading!), I challenge you to think of *Watchman* as you might a complicated and flawed human being. Simple messages and flawless storytelling might define childhood masterpieces, but Lee's parent novel knows that grownups need stories reflective of their imperfect reality, yet respectful of a longing for youth.

How to Get the Most out of This Sidekick

The next two sections of this Sidekick—*Exploring the Author's Fictional World* and *Chapter Analysis & Discussion*—will be most useful <u>while</u> you are reading the novel. You can also refer to the *Character Guide* for a quick "who's who." All subsequent sections—from *A Closer Look* all the way through to *If You Loved This Novel*—are designed to be read <u>after</u> you have finished the novel.

Wherever you are in your reading of the book, with this Sidekick you'll get a chance to dive a little deeper into the author's world, spend some more time with your favorite characters, and check out some of the book's themes and symbolism. There might even be a few Easter eggs along the way.

If you don't have a copy of *Go Set a Watchman* yet, be sure to pick one up before you get started—after all, here be spoilers! (Don't worry, they're clearly marked.) You can order a copy of the novel on Amazon.

* * *

Disclaimer: I'm not Harper Lee. I don't know Harper Lee. Neither I nor WeLoveNovels has any association with Harper Lee whatsoever. What you've got in your hands is 100% independent and unauthorized opinion, commentary, and analysis.

Go Set a Watchman
A Sidekick to the Harper Lee Novel

Exploring the Author's Fictional World

For those who have read *To Kill a Mockingbird*, déjà vu might set in as you note several similar passages within *Go Set a Watchman*. These passages repeat descriptions that reflect what Jean Louise hopes, with increasing desperation, is true: Maycomb, Alabama, and its geography, origin, and character, have not changed since a six year-old kid of the 1930s called it home.

Though a fictional town preoccupies Jean Louise's thoughts, real emotion and experience define her struggle with Lee's setting. The fabricated names of the town and its inhabitants cannot hide their connection to the author's own life: an attorney for a father, a black housekeeper, a friend who visited every summer, and a small Southern town. The very start of our narrative—a young, New York woman returning home—is likewise borne of Lee's experience. Thus, autobiography shapes *Go Set a Watchman,* and reclassifies its musings on challenging subjects like race relations and social expectations as lived experiences and personal struggles.

History too has a role to play. In the novel, Jean Louise will reference bus boycotts and, consequently, your own knowledge of the battle for civil rights in the 1950s will begin to color your perception of this white woman, her Southern hometown, and the conflict that emerges. Maybe your thoughts on recent events, or your own political ideologies will begin to creep in as well. Perhaps you will sympathize or grow angry with Jean Louise, her father, or both. Still, you should (and now will!) remember that Lee wrote a book about a real time and a (almost) real place with problems she witnessed more intimately than most of us ever could. As we head into the book, it's important to remember Lee's closeness to these problems and to this fictional world—while never forgetting that the struggles her characters face are still to be found in our own, very un-fictional, world.

Go Set a Watchman
A Sidekick to the Harper Lee Novel

Chapter Analysis & Discussion

Part I: Chapters 1-3

Consider: a train that literally moves forward in time and in space, but only at the hands of an ever-laughing, unchanging conductor. It's not just the opening image of *Go Set a Watchman*—it's also a symbol of a theme that seems to underlie these first few chapters: the constancy of change. In fact, given the juxtaposition of the detailed description of Maycomb's origin and the simple, stark statement that, "Her father was not waiting for her," *Watchman* seems ready to remind us that the past promises nothing but memories. This early preoccupation with the differences between the past and the present seems eerily self-aware for a book that was written before, yet came long after, literature's first foray into the world of Jean Louise Finch. And yet . . .

Watchman begins as does any other book, and those that have not touched *To Kill a Mockingbird* since their let's-skip-sixth-period selves discovered the movie version likely appreciate the initial setting-the-stage feel of Part I. Even so, surely everyone's mental bells begin to ring as the famed Atticus Finch, a once "big *man*" (emphasis added), reveals that he has two *watches*, one for the present and one from the past.

Beyond this clear connection between Atticus and the past, Part I hints at another potential theme. In this section, we get a brief mention of bus boycotts, a Supreme Court case, and "that Mississippi business" (probably referring to the

brutal murder of fourteen-year-old Emmett Till).
Perhaps those familiar with the racial tensions of
To Kill a Mockingbird will begin to think *plot,
plot, plot!* The novel, however, neither dwells on
these tensions nor offers any additional
information explaining the real word context of
these words.

Though the 1954 case *Brown v. Board of
Education* (ending educational segregation and
rejecting the "separate but equal" philosophy of
the Jim Crow South) is likely the case to which
Atticus refers, we do not really know how he
feels about the decision. His words, "a bid for
immortality," could suggest an excessive
grandiosity or a transcendent wisdom. Similarly,
we do not learn much about Jean Louise's
thoughts on these turbulent events. While her
mention of "bus strikes" suggests that the civil
rights movement serves as the backdrop of
Watchman, these statements are vague and in
passing. Their brief treatment ultimately stands
in contrast to the swaths of text devoted to Jean
Louise's internal judgments and fears
surrounding Aunt Alexandra's prodding. Perhaps
this contrast will become significant, but, until we

read on, we can only wonder at whether the personal or the political will matter more to our protagonist's homecoming.

Part II: Chapters 4-5

These two chapters flit between the past and the present. We see more of the generalized history of Maycomb and glimpse Scout at play, but we also see memories that do not belong to Jean Louise at all. For example, we have Alexandra's recollection of Uncle Jimmy succeeding at the out-of-time, medieval game of jousting and the love it inspired in our (Southern) lady, and we have Henry's sense that the Scout who threw rocks and called out in her fever-induced sleep was and is his. Yet Alexandra and Uncle Jimmy are now estranged, and we're forced to ask how Henry can have ownership over a woman who cannot fully reveal her heart to him. After muttering a few lines of the Matthew Arnold poem "The Buried Life" that describes human inability to know or speak of our inner selves unless in the company of a true lover, Jean Louise chooses not to share her romantic musings with Henry. So, while Henry thinks the past proves Scout as his, Jean Louise

21

of the present daydreams without any playmates, any partners, or any owners.

To steal the lingo of the pseudo-intellectuals you knew in college, the narrative's fluid treatment of past and present is very meta for a book that is and is not a sequel, that is and is not of 2015. Furthermore, this unclear line between past and present also seems to reflect Jean Louise's divided mind, the one that must choose between Maycomb and New York. While we do not yet know where she will settle, the external conflicts of the time—represented by the approaching car of black men—move closer to the internal struggle of Jean Louise. The car appears just as Jean Louise wonders if domestic life in Maycomb will satisfy her, a sign that much as she may dislike politics, she can't have a personal life untouched by the problems unfolding in her hometown.

Part III: Chapters 6-7

Doxology, the book's title, and Uncle Jack?! Allow me to clarify some of what occurs when the Finches go to church. For the non-religious among us, a doxology is simply a short hymn of praises to God. In *Go Set a Watchman*, we see the words of the Common Doxology, so common, in fact, that many Protestants simply call it "The Doxology." The issue over *how* the hymn goes reflects the very real diversity that actually defines the Common Doxology: some Protestant traditions add or eliminate words and adjust its music to match their beliefs and practices. It's an apt metaphor for a single, large country with many contrasting and competing cultures.

Many of the references that Uncle Jack (and, to her credit, Jean Louise) make while complaining about the change in the singing of the hymn are related to hymns or to their composers, but some are not. For example, Jean Louise thinks that her Uncle looks very much like

Theobald Pontifex, a character in the novel *The Way of All Flesh,* a book that attacks Victorian philosophy and chronicles four generations of Pontifexes. Such a story seems highly parallel to that of a young woman forever a part of the South because of her ancestry, yet chafing against the very things she hopes will never change.

But the most "hey-look-at-me" moment of this chapter? "Go set a watchman," revealed at last for the non-religious among us as a biblical passage. Stone's sermon offers little philosophy, but instead tells us a familiar (if formulaic and uncomforting) message that the traditional, the familial, and the communal can order our world and rid us of moral uncertainty. Isaiah 21, on the other hand, tells us of fear, but also of hope. In this biblical passage, those of an evil city (Babylon) that once caused suffering are now seen to suffer, but it terrifies those of the good city. Unsure whether the evil will approach them, the good city's watchman looks out and waits. Finally, he reports that Babylon has fallen. So then does Stone's sermon hold the answer? Is family our watchman? Is family to tell us when evil is coming and, at last, going?

Author Harper Lee's friend and retired history professor Wayne Flynt suggests another interpretation. He believes that Lee considered her hometown (and by extension Jean Louise's Maycomb) to represent Babylon, in that its proclaimed morality and propriety conflicted with its prejudice and injustice. Consequently, the town (fictional and unfictional) needs a watchman to "identify what [its citizens] need to do to get out of [this] mess." Though it's an appealing interpretation, we may not know if Flynt, or Stone, or even we ourselves have understood the watchman until we have turned to the last page of Lee's book.

Part III: Chapters 8-10

Pamphlets like *The Black Plague* were real, and citizens' councils were real, but Atticus Finch, once our beloved champion of justice, is not real. Nonetheless his representation in literature still matters because, as *The Black Plague* pamphlet itself suggests, words and stories have the power to influence both individuals and cultures. Consequently, we should recognize the importance of understanding just what the new (but actually the oldest and original version) of Atticus Finch means both to his daughter and to his readers.

Structurally, Chapter 8 of *Go Set a Watchman* repeats some of its earlier techniques to much greater effect: Jean Louise's internal monologue rides up against a spoken-aloud and fragmented ideology that she hates, but this time that ideology doesn't just impact her aunt's perception of her, but also the perception and treatment of countless other Americans. *Watchman* thus argues that the emotional and the private inform the external and the political even if we do not care or think about such implications. Similarly, the present again informs and re-shapes the past: Jean Louise stands on the "Colored balcony" where she once watched her father win an acquittal for a black man wrongly accused of rape. On the one hand, this simply repeats the technique of having Jean Louise return to a place only to find it not quite as she remembered and cherished. Readers of *To Kill a Mockingbird*, however, will recall that Tom Robinson, the accused and innocent rapist, did not go free. Does this mean that *Mockingbird* got its hero and its story all wrong? Or did *Watchman*? Did the child Scout imagine a story, play make-believe with Jem about the struggles their good father tried and could not overcome? Does *Watchman* want us to consider that an unjust system and a flawed man can do good?

These questions may not have answers, but they're worth considering. And we might find some clues in an unlikely place: the concept of "trash." Both Alexandra and Jean Louise use this term, though they're describing very different stereotypes. In a seemingly unrelated passage,

Jean Louise talks about how she did not know she was a girl, and how she always felt most comfortable away from her peers.

In employing the loaded word "trash," and exposing Jean Louise as once and always an outsider, *Watchman* is pointing out the power of labels. Atticus Finch is a racist, Jean Louise is a girl, and the black man is inferior. Of all these statements, the last has absolutely no merit, and the second, given what we now know about transgender identity and gender stereotypes, likely has no merit except as a term describing biological sex. Where does that leave the first? Are all reductions of identity equal, do all labels dehumanize, and, if so, is all dehumanization, whether systematic or personal, the same?

Part IV: Chapters 11-12

That sentence from the very first chapter, "Her father was not waiting for her," does not just have a metaphorical significance. It also indicates an absence that the novel continues to affirm—first by keeping Atticus largely out of the story, and then by suggesting that he wasn't the only one to raise Scout.

Henry grabs Scout from death, Cal (finally) explains the real facts of life to her, and Jem lets her know that she can come to him with anything, even those things unfit for their father's ears. Yet, "someone had covered her up during the night," and this is likely Atticus. The same father whose anger and disappointment inspired guilt in the otherwise stubborn Scout, the same father who laughed instead of yelled when she flouted Southern propriety, and the same father who sent her away so she could start her own life.

And so we have two versions of Atticus, the absent, racist man and the wise, loving, father. The references to *The Picture of Dorian Grey* in these chapters draws out the fact that Jean Louise has two irreconcilable concepts of the man she loves. Is there comfort in the knowledge that Dorian Grey presented his false, pleasing self to the world and hid his grotesque, true self in a portrait none could see? Has Atticus feigned certain attitudes to appease but still counsel his town? Whether or not that is a morally comforting thought, Atticus, unlike Dorian, does not live selfishly when it comes to his daughter. Perhaps his absence and his willingness to let her become her own, less-than-proper self indicates that he knows he cannot force his ideology on his children.

But while we have a daughter disappointed by her father in these chapters, we cannot end our discussion without acknowledging that we also have a mother disappointed by her almost-daughter. Calpurnia's words, "What are you all doing to us?" is a devastating but important reminder that Jean Louise is not the one most hurt by Atticus's and Hank's racism. In coming after a chapter that focuses upon "the curse of Eve" and the shame of pregnancy, the ability of a woman who personally cared for a child to dismiss her and the ability of a father to falter in his role as moral watchman complicates gender roles by rejecting the traditional understanding of the father as the intellectual, moral, and economic head of the family and the mother as its source of comfort and unconditional love. Consequently, *Watchman* asks to consider whether our politics, or our public, Alexandra-like manners and philosophies, reveal more about our true character than our familial and private kindnesses ever could.

Part V: Chapters 13-14

In Part V of *Go Set a Watchman*, several now-familiar devices let us get inside the head of Jean Louise, and boy did I feel as angry and confused by its end as she seemed.

The dreaded Coffee reintroduces the technique of juxtaposing Jean Louise's inner monologue alongside swatches of conversation from the guests. At the Coffee, however, little tidbits that before only revealed Jean Louise's true responses to what she hears become a window into her distress. For example, a question about New York prompts a complicated, twisted, and emotional inner dialogue that becomes the statement, "New York? It'll always be there." While this verbal answer seems flippant, Jean Louise's thoughts on New York manners again returns us to *Watchman*'s preoccupation with the personal and the public. Manners are expectations guiding our treatment of others, but we, like the girl asking after New York, never know what's going on inside another's head.

This might seem like an simple observation until you examine it against Uncle Jack's reference-filled doozy of a discussion with Jean Louise in the following chapter. We hear about English clergymen who brought the faith to Africa (e.g. Bishop Colenso), we hear of odd, inter-related Maycombers, and we try to guess just who Uncle Jack sees in the mirror. What all of these moments and allusions have in common, though, is that they relate to ideologies and ways of life that struggle to gain influence over a given turf, whether that turf holds a culturally distinct race, supports a society divided by rich and poor, or describes the heart of a girl unsure of who she is and what she believes. Uncle Jack seems to be saying that societies and individuals define themselves by which ideas they choose to accept and which they reject—and that change, whether for good or for evil, always comes at a cost.

Part VI: Chapters 15-17

In Chapter 15, we see Calpurnia, Henry, and Atticus act as Scout's protectors. Calpurnia may anticipate the dangers to come, Atticus may orchestrate the protection needed when they do come, and Henry may do anything at all to keep her safe (so long as it does not jeopardize him), but all have a role to play. While her name and status might give her the freedom to flout convention, Jean Louise still must live with and love those who think that danger in flouting convention exists at all. Whether these are conventions associated with jumping into the river naked, wearing and removing falsies, or standing up against the ideology of her hometown, the Jean Louise of Chapter 16 seems ready to reject her protectors and to challenge Henry's "doing what you don't want to do" philosophy.

Except we have to wonder if she is ready to stand on her own unbothered by the opinions of foe and family. Jean Louise says to Henry that they are "poles apart." Nonetheless, she will not accept that she and her father possess different moral codes. Similarly, she, like Henry, wishes for normalcy and acceptance from her community even if it means she would not be the same Jean Louise: "Why in the name of God didn't you marry again . . . [a] lady who would have raised me right? . . . I'd have been typical one hundred per cent Maycomb." Though she's ready to express her own ideas about systematic inequality (and unfortunately reveal a little of her own distinct and misguided ideas on race), she cannot accept that Atticus will still love her when she despises him. No matter what she thinks of Henry, she and Atticus cannot be "poles apart" . . . right?

Part VII: Chapters 18-19

Here, at last we either confirm our suspicions or release an "a-ha" as Uncle Jack states, "[e]very man's island, Jean Louise, every man's watchman, is his conscience." We may find a copy of the Robert Browning poem *Childe Rolande to the Dark Tower Came*, note the author's description of a modern world that has no adequate spiritual guide, and feel grateful that we have Uncle Jack's words of refutation, his answer to Browning's bleak vision.

Though *Go Set a Watchman* ends with a hopeful resolution (for Jean Louise and her father, though arguably not for Calpurnia and race relations), it likewise leaves us with several unchallenged statements that might not sit easy with all readers. Jean Louise, the bigot? Our protagonist certainly revealed several of what you might call of her time-and-place opinions, but in comparison to her father, the term bigot does not seem to apply. As no character or device undercuts Jack's statement, however, it seems *Watchman* wants us to find virtue in those capable of listening rather than in any one ideology. Similarly, Jack seems to praise Jean Louise's color-blindness, but do we really consider it a virtue that she never once expected Calpurnia to resent her for what her family's privilege represents and has done to the black community?

Though we get to hear the imperfect Atticus champion a daughter willing to go forward and correct what he, the old, has done wrong, we need not close *Go Set a Watchman* and feel content. Instead, we can discuss, we can consider, we can stop to take stock of just what our own conscience, our own watchman, sees.

Go Set a Watchman
A Sidekick to the Harper Lee Novel

Character Guide

Atticus Finch - Father to Jean Louise and an attorney in Maycomb.

Aunt Alexandra - Sister of Atticus Finch and Aunt of Jean Louise

Calpurnia - The Finch's old cook and housekeeper.

Charles "Dill" Baker Harris - Childhood friend of Jean Louise who has traveled to Europe.

Hank "Henry" Clinton - Childhood friend of Jem Finch, apprentice-of-sorts to Atticus Finch, and sometimes flame and potential fiancée of Jean Louise Finch.

Jean Louise "Scout" Finch - Daughter of Atticus Finch.

Jem Finch - Brother of Jean Louise Finch and son of Atticus Finch; deceased.

John "Jack" Hale Finch - Brother to Atticus and Alexandra and Uncle to Jean Louise.

A Closer Look:

Atticus Finch and Jean Louise

As much as Lee makes Scout her protagonist, Atticus Finch and what he represents to the young Jean Louise have consumed readers since the 1960 publication of *To Kill a Mockingbird*. A moment from the first chapter of *Go Set a Watchman* and the ultimate need for Jean Louise to "kill" her father and herself indicates that we must analyze these two together to understand the true implication of this (these) novels.

In Chapter 1, Jean Louise discusses how she has lost contact with almost all of her childhood friends, and I, as a reader of *Mockingbird* and a lover of children's literature, felt these words had a special significance. The childhood of Scout may have felt special to the reader, and may even have led that reader to feel, as Henry did, ownership over the girl who would forever stay young and feisty. *Watchman*, however, is here to tell us that kids grow up and become their own masters, and we, whether readers of the "parent" book or as parents like Atticus, must let them.

The notion of killing both the father and the self recalls Freud and the ideas he named after the myth of a man destined to marry his mother and kill his father. That theory and that myth are remarkable for many reasons, but particularly with respect to this story because both imply that our parents shape who we are, whether or not we ever find out. (Freud believed children are born without identity and must learn to think of themselves as separate beings; Oedipus fulfils his destiny because he does not know his true identity.) The violence Freud's theoretical, "separated" child feels toward the parent and

Oedipus's decision to gouge his own eyes out upon realizing he has killed his father and married his mother ultimately align with *Watchman's* notion that violence and trauma define growing up.

So, Atticus' general absence from the memories of *Watchman* and his decision to not fight back with his true and full opinion may very well mean that *Mockingbird* and *Watchman* do not want us to debate the heroism of a racist man. Instead, *Watchman* might ask us to debate the significance of a woman who hates racism but who reveals some racist attitudes herself, of a woman who has accepted her femininity but still defies its stereotypes, of a woman, unlike her parent Atticus, still preoccupied with the self.

Aunt Alexandra

Aunt Alexandra is "the last of her kind," a woman who does not feel—or so says Jean Louise. But can this woman, or anybody for that matter, really have paid no "emotional bills" in her lifetime?

We get two clues in the early chapters of *Go Set a Watchman* that Jean Louise has misunderstood her aunt. First, we have Jean Louise saying that Alexandra cared not at all when she and her husband separated, but we see Alexandra become very concerned with Jean Louise deciding to tie herself to someone. While that may simply reinforce Jean Louise's my-aunt's-an-uptight-snob diatribe, another early clue counters that interpretation. The act that disarms even Jean Louise: her aunt's decision to move in with her father, allowing Jean Louise to remain in New York, suggests there's something soft behind Alexandra's stiff moral rectitude.

In fact, we get direct evidence later in the novel showing us that Alexandra feels, perhaps with even more sensitivity than one like Jean Louise used to hearing the negativity of her Aunt's shoulds and should nots. When she begins to cry upon hearing Jean Louise's criticism, we realize that her well-mannered exterior plays much the same function as Calpurnia's "company manners": it serves as both a shield from the world and an acknowledgement that the personal, emotional, maybe even feral Scout-like instinct may not be enough to navigate it. So, in a way Alexandra is more human than Jean Louise allows. Yet at the same time, this very humanness also makes her into something of a symbol, rather than a living, breathing person—a symbol that *Watchman* uses to communicate its thoughts on the external and the internal, the political and the personal.

Go Set a Watchman
A Sidekick to the Harper Lee Novel

Imagining Alternate Endings

While our protagonist does decide to love her father, we do not get an answer to another question asked throughout the novel: Maycomb or New York? *Go Set a Watchman* could have ended with a choice, a choice that made its thoughts on Southern culture, racism, and the duty of a woman like Scout clear:

They Lived Happily Ever After

Henry believes that he must pretend to fit in and become perfect in the eyes of Maycomb in order to escape his trash past and make a difference. Interestingly, Uncle Jack believes something similar of Jean Louise: she must return to her home and blend into its ways because they need her to change those ways. We readers know that Jean Louise's "color-blindness" does not really work because race exists and defines us in ways that require dialogue and understanding, but might Jean Louise return, become a politician's wife, and serve as the Atticus Finch of her generation? Could she become the more progressive, yet still imperfect beacon of hope for a just future? At the very least, this ending of *Watchman* certainly would express its belief in the possibility of change.

The Prodigal Daughter (Never) Returns

If Uncle Jack hadn't stopped Jean Louise, it's easy to imagine she would have left, as promised, never to return. Atticus, Henry, and Maycomb would become memories, much like Jem and Dill have. New York would probably never feel like home, as Jean Louise is as much an outsider there as she was among those who enjoy the Coffees. New York, however, would challenge her, form her into a person who cared very much about politics and about a world beyond herself. Atticus would eventually die, and she would be sad, but she would still not go home. For her, Maycomb would be an unreal world now. She would become like many, desperate for a different South, but content to pretend that the "trash" viewpoints of the world are not real, and that the people who hold them are not real human beings who change and grow.

Go Set a Watchman
A Sidekick to the Harper Lee Novel

Themes & Symbols You May Have Missed

Ice Cream and its Rumpelstiltskin

The dream-like interlude in which Jean Louise wanders through an empty Maycomb and winds up at the ice cream parlor that has replaced her childhood home screams symbolism. Reality seems to distort during these two hours, complete with a man jokingly called Rumpelstiltskin. It only returns with the of-course revelation that this man is a Cunningham. In the fairytale of Rumpelstiltskin, a young woman must guess a stranger's name correctly; if she fails, she must give him her firstborn child. In a sort of funhouse reflection of the tale, Jean Louise finds herself searching for some kind of answer that will keep her from losing her father—at least, the father she thought she knew.

Dreams and fairytales, like childhood, end, but those who grow up stay connected to their past and to their names. The interlude itself invites a similar realization as Jean Louise allows her white ice cream to melt. She remarks that she did that, and we know that her lost innocence (represented by the spilled whiteness) was and is not just something that happens, but something all children should and do seek out. When they return to the past, its reality is a gone, but a fairytale, a dream, or a memory of happiness and ice cream remains.

Uncle Jack and Literary Allusions

Clearly, Harper Lee read a book or two before writing *Go Set a Watchman*. While exploring allusions almost always enhances literary analysis, I have to wonder if there's something more to their inclusion in *Go Set a Watchman* given their prevalence in the novel and given the decision to create a character as well-read as Uncle Jack. At the novel's conclusion, we come to see Uncle Jack as a champion of Southern nationalism, a believer in history's enduring significance, and a member of a more inclusive, less normative family (where it's okay to love your brother's wife and consider his children your own). Many of the poems, novels, and writers mentioned in *Watchman* reference the very themes Uncle Jack represents.

Consider *The Strange Case of Alger Hiss*, the book that Atticus reads with displeasure because it seems "like Fenimore Cooper writin' *The Waverley Novels*." Though it's a head-scratching reference for someone not living in the early 1900s, a little research indicates that Atticus states this because he feels strongly about just who gets to remember and define the past. An Earl of England (William Jowitt) published *The Strange Case of Alger Hill* in 1953 to describe the title character's conviction as a perjured communist spy. America's first national novelist, Fenimore Cooper, may have copied the romance and adventure model of *Waverly's* author (Sir Walter Scott) to create 1820s fiction about the American frontier—but he didn't go so far as to write historical novels set in Scotland and England. You might also realize that many of the books referenced or read, like *The Reason Why* or *The Picture of Dorian Grey*, occur in the Victorian age, a time when old notions of love, class, morality, identity, and life were fast disappearing.

These references, together with the outspoken man who would recognize every single one of them, suggest that maybe *Watchman* wants us to remember that its racial conflict does not just belong to a specific time and place. Instead, Lee connects the turmoil in the South to the conflict that has always existed whenever groups of people divide and fix upon certain ways to live and come to believe that those ways can never—and should never—change.

Stark Naked

We see Scout "in the stark" in Jean Louise's memory and we hear, wrongly, of the present Jean Louise "in the stark" while swimming with a man. If anything screams purposeful in a novel, repetition of language and image within a two-chapter span certainly does. Nakedness evokes many things, and here specifically it calls to mind Scout's innocence (think Adam and Eve, pre-apple) and conservative Maycomb's values (think *The Scarlet Letter* but ignore New England). Jean Louise is no longer an innocent child—she easily jokes about what adult nakedness implies—but she was not naked in that water either. Placed alongside Scout's mock baptism, the Maycomb gossip about Jean Louis and Henry suggests that she has not yet fully grown into her own adult self.

Watchman's Controversy in Today's Publishing Industry

John Green, the YouTube star; J.K. Rowling, happy to delight the public with a biting tweet; and Harper Lee, refusing to give interviews after the success of *To Kill a Mockingbird*? Today's publishing industry—and the opportunity and threat that the Internet as a promoter and a usurper of good books presents—does not resemble the one in which Lee first introduced Jean Louise "Scout" Finch to the world. Today, blogs, behind-the-scenes tidbits, "likes," and big personalities matter almost as much as the story itself, particularly in the realm of children's literature where an obsessive fan reaction may seem more age appropriate and, more importantly, easier to manipulate and commercialize (think action hero movie, action hero figurine, action hero Halloween costume, action hero birthday plates, and on and on and on).

Lee's reclusiveness, alongside her failing health, the death of her primary attorney, caregiver, and sister, and her fifty-five-year promise to never publish again, raised concern about the supposed discovery and subsequent publication of *Go Set a Watchman*. The media has described how her other attorney found a manuscript she assumed was an early draft of *Mockingbird*, the eventual realization that it was another, different book, and the subsequent decision to publish what *The New York Times* has deemed one of the most important discoveries in contemporary American literature. Shock that this discovery took over half a century, and Lee's particular character and current physical state led many to cry "elder abuse," but Lee herself silenced the naysayers with a statement expressing her satisfaction that the book she thought long lost would meet the public at last.

The truth in that statement, or in the book's tale of discovery (akin to finding buried treasure hiding in your average safe deposit box) does not really capture the "why" of this media circus. Store openings at midnight, the most pre-ordered book on Amazon since the final installment of *Harry Potter*—very few books garner this kind of public interest. In fact, publishing any book to widespread success in the post-Internet age has become much more difficult absent built-in fanfare. But a shocking revelation about one of the most beloved fictional characters of American literature, an odd look-what-we-found-by-someone-who-swore-never-to-publish-again story, a conspiracy theory, and a twenty-four-hour news cycle to boot? Such is fanfare in its own right, and ultimately should maybe suggest to the quieter writers of our world that they need not fret. Some publisher might just concoct a marketing strategy capable of overcoming their technology-challenged, mousey persona that is nonetheless worthy of their transformational prose.

The Big Picture: What can we take away from this novel?

Police brutality, cultural appropriation, and random acts of violence have dominated our news cycle of late. The face of racial tension in America may mean something different in 2015, but it nonetheless exists as much as it did when Jean Louise returned home to Maycomb, Alabama in the 1950s.

Consequently, the timing of *Go Set a Watchman*'s discovery and the themes it ultimately conveys seem almost too perfectly parallel to our world to ignore. How can we not use it as tool to understand the Atticus, the Henry, the Jean Louise, and the Calpurnia of our world?

Today, the impoverished we call "white trash," the suit-and-tie lawyer calling for deportation and voter ID cards, the liberal millennial who rarely heads to the polls, the kid from the hood with no family or opportunity, and the girl who watches the television without ever seeing a face like hers all call the same country home and all, in some way, resemble the characters of *Go Set a Watchman*. We could use "trash" or any other slur to describe these individuals, and we could walk away from them, as Jean Louise does from Calpurnia, when they say something too hard or too awful or too ignorant. On the other hand, we could listen. We could try to learn from our mistakes, to open our eyes to our own prejudices—and to believe that communication holds more hope than dismissal.

Go Set a Watchman
A Sidekick to the Harper Lee Novel

Possible Storylines for a Prequel

In a book that is at once a sequel and a prequel of *To Kill a Mockingbird, Go Set a Watchman* may offer us less potential storyline possibilities than other, stand-alone novels. The possibilities we do have, however, would likely prove as deep and as rich as the countless literary allusions Lee threw into the three-hundred-some pages of *Watchman*.

Scout or Jean Louise?

In an interview regarding *Go Set a Watchman*, Harper Lee's agent revealed that the author had intended to create a trilogy with *Mockingbird*, another book, and *Watchman*. Though *Watchman* shows some of the struggles Jean Louise has faced in recognizing and adapting to her own femininity, Lee does not elaborate much upon the years in which her protagonist pretended to like the makeup and boy-driven gossip of her peers. Similarly, little explanation is given for her dislike of her women's college. A middle novel in which Scout becomes Jean Louise and struggles to understand what being a woman means in the forties and fifties would thus prove fascinating, both as a character study and as a larger commentary on gender.

The Children of Jean Louise Finch

A sequel to *Watchman*, set perhaps twenty years in the future, would allow us to witness the formation and separation of Jean Louise's children from their mother (and father), and perhaps to learn a little something about progress along the way. The slow but inevitable march of change would continue, and we might even feel like we were reading *The Way of All Flesh* (the story detailing the lives of four generations referenced by Uncle Jack) as we read this latest installment alongside its predecessors.

It seems quite likely that Jean Louise's son and daughter would embrace the peace, love, anti-war, and anti-establishment ethos of their time. While Jean Louise—the tomboyish, always-in-trouble Scout of earlier days—would understand the need to rebel and sympathize with the dislike of big government, she would also worry that her children might reject the normative family lifestyle she had loved and, because of the death of her mother, the death of her brother, and her decision to move away, lost. While her children would be younger than the draft-card-burning and commune-joining young adults of the sixties and seventies, their political awakening (and, at times, dangerous attempts to participate in the resistance of the older kids) would stir up hard questions and deep concerns for the mother who disagreed with, yet loved, her father—the woman who hates change, yet cannot agree with society's norms.

In the Final Analysis . . .

Many might consider *Go Set a Watchman* a difficult book. The narrative jumps in time and does not reveal its central conflict until Chapter 8. Throw in a few odd allusions to books that those of this century likely have not read, and craft a point of view that jarringly, almost randomly jumps from the protagonist to others within the novel, and you can safely conclude that this novel has certain structural oddities. Yet, for both *Mockingbird* lovers and mere acquaintances of the name Atticus Finch, the most difficult part of *Watchmen* remains its role in distorting a figure of American culture.

Since they have cracked the spine of this tale from Harper Lee, critics have compared *Watchman* to *Mockingbird*, lamented it as lesser in style, and mourned its figurative murder of the old Atticus Finch. This reader, however, challenges those critics. Yes, this novel has a complicated, even difficult structure, but one of purpose, seeking to remind us that the past, the present, and our perception color every moment of our lives. Yes, this novel has changed how we view Atticus Finch, but uncomplicated characters should not our models make. Of course, neither should racists, but we should recognize and talk about good, yet flawed human beings much more than we do fictional heroes. Malcom Gladwell recognized Finch as one unwilling to crusade against the Jim Crow South long before *Watchman* surfaced, and perhaps we should have known too and always discussed him as such.

Or maybe we should avoid this to-do about Atticus Finch entirely, and instead take in the message of Lee's new-old novel by setting our own watchman, by looking out to see what evil lurks in our own society, and by listening to those who ask, "What are you all doing to us?" *Go Set a Watchman* highlights Jean Louise's political apathy and personal absorption much more than it does the nature of Atticus' racism. Maybe it does so with the hope that our own watchman will recognize that as the greatest evil in the novel—and in ourselves.

Go Set a Watchman
A Sidekick to the Harper Lee Novel

If You Loved This Novel . . .

To Kill a Mockingbird by Harper Lee

If you have *not* read Harper Lee's only other novel, *To Kill A Mockingbird*, it deserves a spot on your reading list. *Mockingbird* chronicles the coming of age of a young, tomboyish girl as her father and idol, Atticus Finch, defends a black man accused of raping a white woman in the Jim Crow South. Not only does *Mockingbird* make for an amazing read in its own right—it will also enhance your appreciation of *Watchman's* ability to expose ideology as complicated, rather than simple; character as in progress, rather than fixed; and novel writing as the product of contradictory thought and collaboration, rather than the result of a single idea or a solitary author.

In Cold Blood by Truman Capote

Dill, who visits in the summer; Dill, who feigns a convincing seizure; Dill, who throws a sheet over his head and calls himself the Holy Spirit—this beloved character didn't just walk out of Harper Lee's imagination, but walked into her life as the young boy who would become the famed author Truman Capote. The two remained friends for many years, and Lee even travelled to Kansas with Capote to help him to conduct research for his novel *In Cold Blood*. (Capote, an eccentric and openly gay man in the 1950s, knew that strangers might find him off-putting, and enlisted Lee's help to get Holcomb-ers talking.) One of Capote's most famous works, *In Cold Blood* details a quadruple murder that occurred in Holcomb, Kansas in November of 1959. In meticulously describing the murderers, robbery, and violence that befell a prosperous farm family, Capote created, as he himself stated, the first "nonfiction novel."

Between the World and Me by Ta-Nehisi Coates

Though not Southern, female, or a child in the 1930s, Ta-Nehisi Coates has something to say that will inform how you view Jean Louise's experience in *Go Set a Watchman*. *Watchman* distills the revelation of Atticus' racism, the imperfect progressivism of Jean Louise's "color blind" point of view, and the race relations of Maycomb through the narration and internal thoughts of white characters. *Between the World and Me* offers us commentary on race relations and white responses by presenting itself as a letter from the author to his teenage son on the reality of being black in America. Not optimistic that social change has or will ever occur, Coates's work will either resonate or polarize. It will also remind you that Calpurnia and her grandson have their own thoughts and their own Maycomb to share.

The Help by Kathryn Stockett

A tale of 1960s Mississippi, an independent young woman, and the maids who raised her should have a thematic connection to *Go Set a Watchman*, right? On its surface, sure, but dig deeper and a glaring thematic *dis*connection will emerge. Though many have read this popular novel (or seen the movie), I urge all—new to the story or not— to read the story with Calpurnia's devastating, "What are you all doing to us?" in mind. Remember her words, wonder what the compassionate Scouts of the world should do, and consider whose story needs telling and by whom as you read of this white protagonist and the community of maids who unite to write a book that exposes the racism of families who employ "the help."

So, What'd You Think?

Thanks for investing in this *Sidekick*. Now that you've read it, let us hear from you!

In just a sentence or two, please email founders@welovenovels.com your answer to one simple question:

What was your favorite (or least favorite) thing about this Sidekick?

We want to know what you think, so we can bring you more of what you love most, and fix what you don't like.

And if you would like a free copy of Katherine Miller's top-rated *Sidekick* to *Leaving Time,* Jodi Picoult's latest bestseller, we'd like to send it to you (a $4.99 value). All you have to do is add the words "**Yes, I Want My Bonus Sidekick**" to the email subject line, and you'll get instant access.

About the Author of This Sidekick

Allison grew up in Seattle, WA, and Philadelphia, PA, and studied English and film and media studies at Georgetown University. Upon confronting the post-collegiate "real world," she knew she needed to find a way to continue analyzing (and enjoying!) novels on a regular basis. Consequently, she is excited to share her thoughts with you.

Other Sidekicks from WeLoveNovels

Sidekick to All the Lights We Cannot See

Sidekick to The Martian

Sidekick to The Nightingale

Sidekick to Wayward

Sidekick to Seveneves

Sidekick to Departure

Sidekick to Orphan Train

Sidekick to Gathering Prey

Sidekick to Pines

Sidekick to Memory Man

Sidekick to The Shadows

Sidekick to The Husband's Secret

Sidekick to A Spool of Blue Thread

Sidekick to The DUFF

Sidekick to Insurgent

Sidekick to Redeployment

Sidekick to The Girl on the Train

Sidekick to Still Alice

Sidekick to Captivated by You

Sidekick to Catching Fire

Sidekick to Mockingjay

Sidekick to Deadline

Sidekick to Big Little Lies

Sidekick to Gone Girl

We are so grateful to all who have taken a moment to leave a quick review of one of our Sidekicks on Amazon. Your thoughtfulness means a lot and helps us, and the rest of the world, know how we are doing and how we can improve. :)

Questions? Ideas? Comments?

Email **founders@welovenovels.com**.

We are listening!

Go Set a Watchman
A Sidekick to the Harper Lee Novel

Go Set a Watchman
A Sidekick to the Harper Lee Novel

Go Set a Watchman
A Sidekick to the Harper Lee Novel

Made in the USA
Middletown, DE
04 December 2015